1st Edition
THE TEXAS WHITE HOUSE

Russ Whitlock

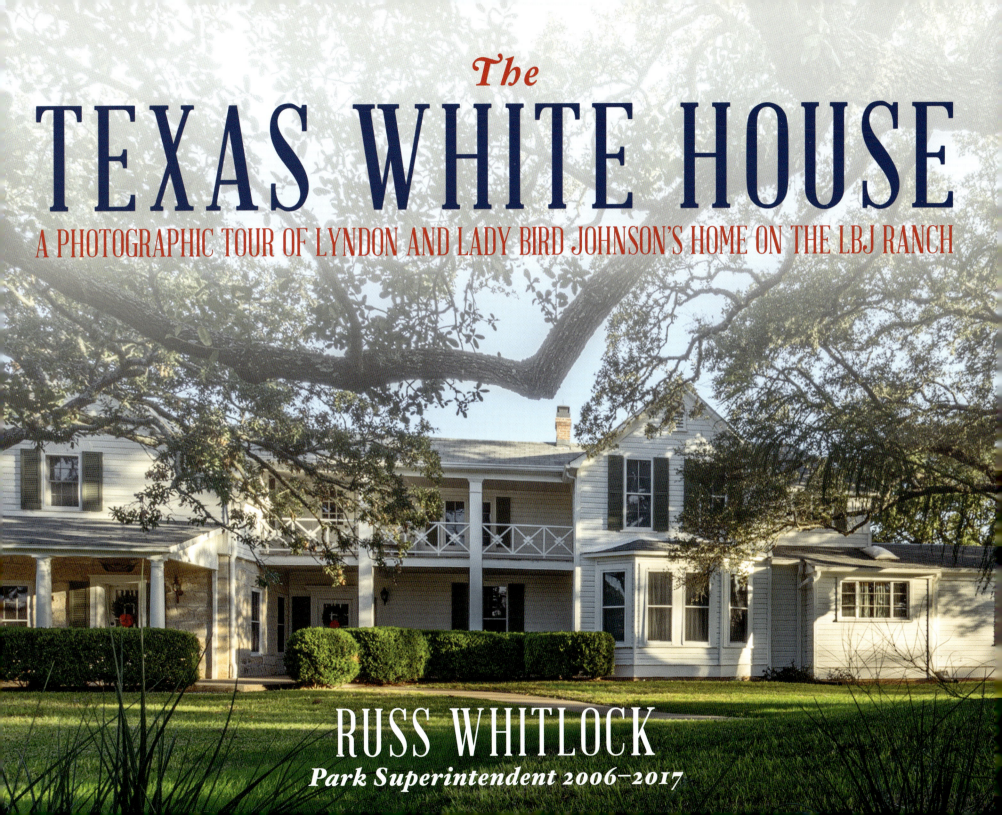

The TEXAS WHITE HOUSE

A PHOTOGRAPHIC TOUR OF LYNDON AND LADY BIRD JOHNSON'S HOME ON THE LBJ RANCH

RUSS WHITLOCK
Park Superintendent 2006–2017

Palmetto Publishing Group
Charleston, SC

The Texas White House
Narrative Text © 2018 by Russ Whitlock. All rights reserved.
Introduction Text © 2018 by Luci Baines Johnson. All rights reserved.
Scot Miller Photographs © 2018. All rights reserved.

David Valdez Photographs in public domain from collection sponsored by Lyndon B. Johnson
National Historical Park and Friends of LBJ National Historical Park.

Photographs in public domain from collection at LBJ Presidential Library.

Photographs courtesy of Shelton Coleman.

Photographs in public domain from Lyndon B. Johnson National Historical Park.

All rights reserved. No part of this book may be reproduced in any
form, by mimeograph, photocopying, digitally, or any other means,
without permission in writing from the authors.

Printed in the United States of America.

ISBN-13: 978-1-64111-142-3
ISBN-10: 1-64111-142-9

FOREWORD

Welcome to the LBJ Ranch!

When I encounter visitors to the ranch that was the home of our family since I was a little girl, I often ask them, "Are you paying your taxes?" Many look like deer in headlights, fearful of where this question is going. But when I encourage them to speak forthrightly, they nod their heads affirmatively, and I say simply, "Welcome home! The LBJ Ranch is as much your home as it is mine!"

On December 22, 1972, my father sat with me at the ranch and shared that he and my mother had given our family home to the American people. My reaction was stunned acceptance. He did this in the nick of time, as he died January 22, 1973. Over the years my children and grandchildren have questioned, "How could you let Boppa do that?" My only response is "This is obvious. You didn't really know your Boppa." My parents wisely did not consult my sister or me about gifting our ranch home to the American people. If they had, we would likely have selfishly begged them to save the place for us. But they knew what we have come to know; our home should belong to the American people.

Daddy thought he was likely to be the last president from the land. That was not meant to be, as he shares that rural heritage with President Carter. But my father thought it was important for Americans to be able to see, to touch, to know firsthand the home of a person who had grown up from humble beginnings to become president of the United States. Education was my father's passport out of poverty. He worked all of his adult life to make that true for all Americans. His administration was all about obtaining social justice through laws that provided opportunities and equality for all Americans in the areas of education (from preschool through university), civil rights (by providing equal access to public accommodations, voting rights, and fair housing), health care through Medicare and Medicaid, consumer affairs, the environment, the arts and humanities, immigration, public broadcasting, space—and the list goes on and on.

My father felt that "the Hill Country of Texas was where people knew when you were sick and cared when you died." He wanted this neighborly compassion to be not just his but the inheritance of all Americans! We hope as you tour what came to be known as the Texas White House that you will feel as Mother always said: "All the world is welcome here." The Johnson family hopes when you leave the ranch you will be inspired, as my father was, to do your part for a more just America.

—Luci Baines Johnson

PAINTING OF LBJ RANCH HOUSE ON A CHAIR IN PRESIDENTIAL SERIES MANUFACTURED BY THE HITCHCOCK CHAIR COMPANY OF CONNECTICUT.

PREFACE

The LBJ Ranch and Texas White House are as synonymous with Lyndon B. Johnson as civil rights, education, and the Vietnam War. This place helped define him and brought him great comfort during the most trying times of his life. The "big house," as the home was called in Johnson's youth, was owned by relatives far more well-off than the Johnsons. It was a place for family gatherings and holiday celebrations, the place a young boy loved and eventually made his own. I heard his daughters often quote their father saying, "The best fertilizer of a man's land is the footsteps of its owner."

A ranger I worked with liked to say, "There is a power of place." Surely that applies to many historic places, but in my years working and tending to this national historical park, I certainly felt a presence, an importance in history, and a satisfaction that the buildings and lands of this park held a special presence and feeling worthy of being conserved and shared. All who inquire and learn about Lyndon and Lady Bird Johnson and the events and decisions that occurred here have the opportunity to pause and experience the power of this place.

This book of pictures includes stories I learned from the people who knew the Johnsons. Your tour through this book is from the perspective of a park superintendent who shares a close friendship with the Johnson family. Mrs. Johnson was the victim of a stroke that took her ability to speak. But during my last visit with her, when we spoke of visitors touring the ranch and home she loved, her reaction was a big smile and clapping hands. I believe this national park, along with over seventy others created or enlarged during the presidency of Lyndon B. Johnson, is another contribution toward his vision of a "Great Society."

The majority of photographs are by Scot Miller, Artist-in-Park at the Lyndon B. Johnson National Historical Park from 2008 through 2017. You can view more of his LBJ Ranch photographs at ScotMiller.com. Former White House photographer David Valdez's work is featured, as well as historic photography compliments of the LBJ Presidential Library and the personal collection of Shelton Coleman. I am grateful to friends at the Lyndon B. Johnson National Historical Park who helped fill in missing images.

—Russ Whitlock

This photograph shows President Johnson playing his favorite game of Dominoes. From the time of his youth, he had found joy at "the big house" on the Pedernales River where his uncle Clarence and aunt Frank Martin lived. Memories of family gatherings would remain with him throughout his adult life, and the LBJ Ranch would provide respite, comfort, reflection, and inspiration. It would become, very much, a working ranch and a source of tremendous pride for him.

In his book LBJ's Texas White House, author Hal Rothman writes, "The ranch had political and personal meaning for Senator Johnson. Wealthy Texans always had ranch property, and in the Senate owning an estate was always an asset. As Johnson emerged as a force in the Senate, the ranch served as a combination of confidence builder and calling card that helped him announce his arrival."

Senator Lyndon B. Johnson and Lady Bird purchased the ranch house and two hundred acres of land from his Aunt Frank Martin, who lived out the rest of her life in the Johnson City home where Lyndon grew up.

Family stories indicate Mrs. Johnson was initially not thrilled with the purchase. She was worried about the financial and personal drain the house and lands would have on the young family already dividing their time between Austin and Washington, DC. Later, Mrs. Johnson would often refer to the beloved ranch and house as "their heart's home."

LYNDON, LADY BIRD, LYNDA, AND LUCI AT THE RANCH HOUSE, DECEMBER 1953.

The ranch house of 1951 included two gables and a two-story porch nestled under expanding live oaks providing almost continuous shade in the front yard. The yard with ranch house as backdrop would become a familiar sight to Americans throughout the 1960s. Press conferences, meetings, social events, and family gatherings regularly occurred in that iconic setting.

THE LBJ RANCH

AERIAL VIEW OF THE RANCH, AUGUST 1968.

From 1951 to 1973, Lyndon and Lady Bird increased the ranch and other land holdings and interests from the initial two hundred acres to over six thousand, according to Lyndon Nugent, the president's grandson. The ranch house, known as Headquarters, would grow from a three-bedroom, two-bath home to include the eight bedrooms and eight and one-half bathrooms you see today. As Lyndon and Lady Bird Johnson increased in wealth and stature, the ranch grew with them. When he became president, reporters covering his frequent trips from Washington to the Texas Hill Country would begin referring to the residence as the Texas White House.

LBJ riding Silver Jay using the ornate saddle gifted by Mexican president Lopez Mateos. "Nita" is Anita Winters of Johnson City. Anita and M.C. Winters were good friends of the Johnsons.

Walking the grounds of the LBJ Ranch, you cover the same footsteps of presidents, astronauts, world leaders, movie stars, and family and friends of the United States representative, senator, vice president, and thirty-sixth president of the United States. Throughout history presidents have enjoyed retreating to family homes or places that have personal meaning for them. President Washington often returned to Mount Vernon. Franklin D. Roosevelt spent as much time as possible at his "Little White House" in Warm Springs, Georgia. John F. Kennedy preferred the Kennedy compound in Hyannis, Massachusetts, and Dwight Eisenhower made repeated visits to his farm at Gettysburg.

Senator Lyndon B. Johnson at main gate to their ranch, November 1958.

As president, LBJ would return home over four hundred times, spending almost fourteen months of his five years in office administering the nation from the LBJ Ranch. When the president was in residence, the world followed. The daily diaries show a calendar filled with meetings and calls functioning as if he were in the Oval Office. Technological advancements in aircraft and communications systems allowed him to operate from remote Texas as if he were in Washington, DC. But here, Johnson could hold meetings under the mighty oaks, beside the swimming pool, or while riding around the ranch pointing out his prize-winning Hereford cattle.

Walking to the ranch house from the Hangar, you pass the communications trailers that housed the switchboard, offices, and assistants, as well as the original Martin Barn. The Klein Shop (named for long-serving ranch maintenance man Lawrence Klein) replaced a set of corrals when the cattle operation was moved to the Show Barn at the top of the hill. The small house holding United States Secret Service offices was moved to the ranch in the late 1950s and originally served as quarters for ranch hands.

The Friends of LBJ National Historical Park and National Park Service enlarged the Hangar (which housed press conferences, parties, movie showings, and the wedding of a Johnson granddaughter) to create a visitor center and exhibit area. One of LBJ's JetStar aircraft was returned to the ranch in 2010. LBJ referred to the JetStar as "Air Force One-Half." Ranch hands still maintain pastures and agricultural fields as they were traditionally cultivated.

As you approach the Texas White House, your first view is of the large stone wall and chimney of the president's office. The two-story stone wall is part of the original house built in the mid-1890s by the Meir family, who were German immigrants to the Hill Country. These thick, hand-hewn limestone blocks have sheltered the occupants and provided a safe and comfortable environment for generations of families and their guests. The stately oaks, so prominent in the yard, have supplied shade for hundreds of years.

THE ORIGINAL HOUSE, 1894/1895.

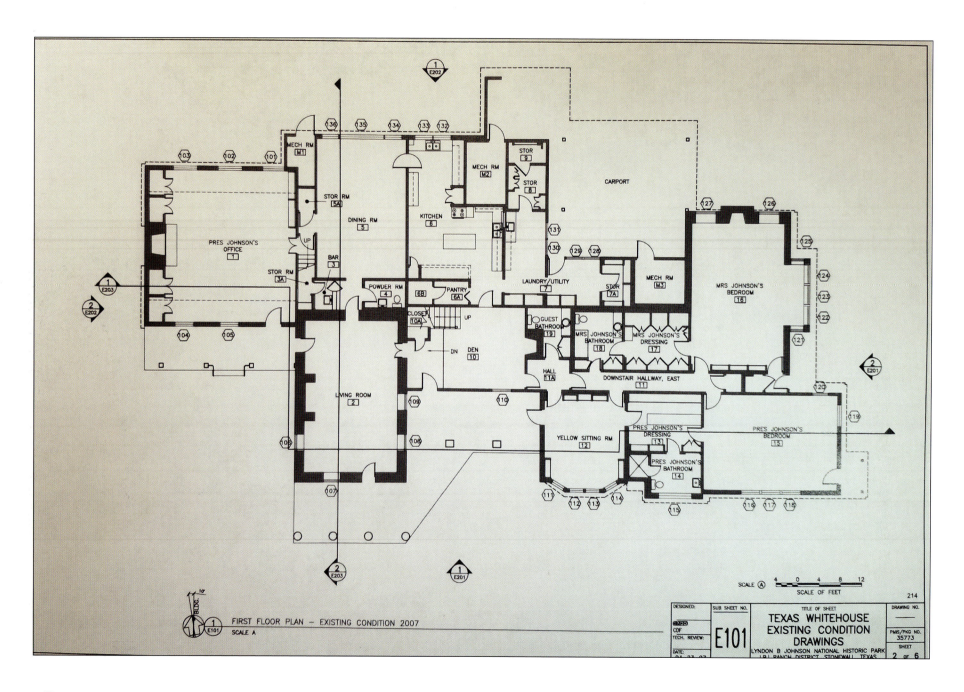

THE FIRST FLOOR

PRESIDENT'S OFFICE

21

View from the president's desk during the Christmas season.

The president's office today is very similar to what you would have experienced in the 1960s, but for people huddled in conversation, sounds of typewriters, a TV news program, and phones ringing. Mrs. Johnson initiated this office addition in 1958 while Lyndon was Senate majority leader. She had grown weary of bedroom meetings and calls at all hours of the night and morning. Her husband was a workaholic, and she tried to provide a location where he and his staff could focus on work. Unfortunately, the new office still did not keep LBJ from conducting business in every room of the house.

The National Park Service painstakingly returned this room to its appearance of the presidential years. Thanks to Lady Bird's forethought, every piece of furniture, the curtains, the light fixtures, and other objects were stored for future use. She was a great proponent of the national parks and knew one day visitors to the ranch would enjoy seeing the room as guests of the president and Mrs. Johnson would have known it.

Many head-of-state gifts remain in the residence on loan from the National Archives. The ornamental saddle was a gift of President Lopez Mateos of Mexico during a visit to the ranch in 1959. On the bookcase behind the president's desk is a Viking funerary axe dating to 2500 BC, a gift of the prime minister of Denmark.

There is a small model of the first Telstar satellite. Vice President Johnson participated in the first satellite-relayed phone call. One hundred one-dollar bills with LBJ's, not Washington's, face are set in an acrylic block, a gift of former Texas governor and then secretary of the treasury John Connally. The flintlock rifle was a gift of C. R. Smith, president of American Airlines, who served as LBJ's secretary of commerce.

The paintings of "Him" and "Her," the Johnson beagles who were part of the White House family, were commissioned by Barbara Streisand and gifted to the president. His desk was a gift from the Senate when he became vice president.

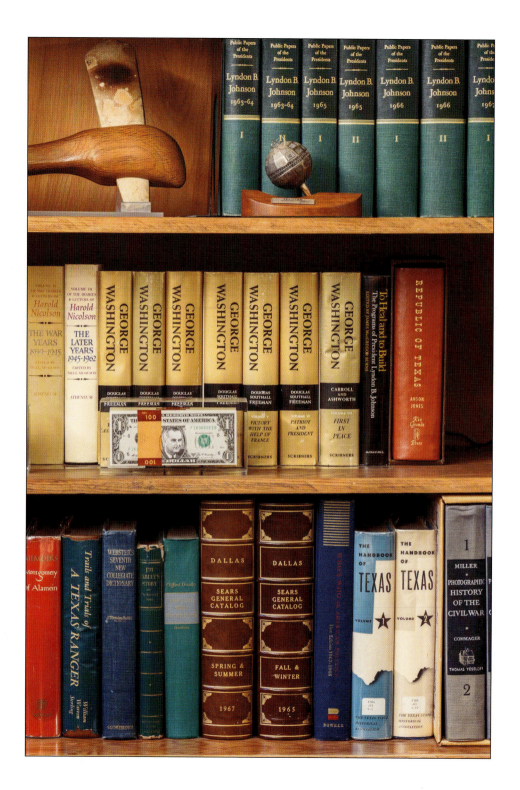

Notice the large painting of Lyndon B. Johnson above the fireplace. This portrait was made in 1959 when he was Senate majority leader.

Luci Johnson shares, "Some of Daddy's happiest days were in the Senate, where he is remembered as the most effective majority leader of his time.

"While his legislative accomplishments as president included landmark legislation such as Medicare, Medicaid, the Elementary and Secondary Education Act, civil rights and voting rights, fair housing, national arts and humanities, and public broadcasting, Daddy was painfully unable to resolve the Vietnam issue, though he endlessly tried to do so."

Lynda Johnson Robb shared that "Daddy always kept a bust of President Eisenhower on the bookshelf behind his desk." He used it to remind others that a Republican president and Democratic Senate majority leader could work well together and frequently find common ground on issues important to the nation.

A pillow in the office, according to Luci Johnson, was "one of Daddy's favorite possessions." It was a gift of Helene Lindow, one of Mrs. Johnson's assistants.

Luci explains, "Helen was fearful President Johnson would find the slogan unbecoming, but was encouraged to give it. It turned out to be Daddy's favorite Christmas present that year. He admonished us all if the house caught fire please make sure you retrieve the pillow."

Mrs. Johnson converted the office to a family room in the years after LBJ's death. Luci has special memories of this room, as she and husband Ian Turpin were married here in 1984. There were three great-grandchildren baptized in the west room.

LIVING ROOM

Mrs. Johnson once stated that she wondered what the leaders of the world thought when they visited the president's home along the banks of the Pedernales River. She felt the living room was the heart of the house, and it was her favorite room. Entering the living room, you are immediately taken by its warm and relaxed feel; there are no crystal chandeliers or rich furnishings. This room, like others throughout the house, is very comfortable and a great reflection of the occupants.

ENTERTAINING ISRAELI PRIME MINISTER LEVI ESHKOL IN THE TEXAS WHITE HOUSE LIVING ROOM.

A large fireplace easily warms the room. A young Lyndon Johnson, as well as his grandchildren, used the fireplace hearth to stage family Christmas productions. Luci's piano holds its place in the corner with a Horacio painting from the president of Mexico on the wall above. In the front corner is a cupboard from the president of Finland. The wall clock is made of wood from Mrs. Johnson's grandmother's home in Autauga County, Alabama. Mrs. Johnson enjoyed collecting copper accessories. Some of the copper is "local," made at a public works facility in nearby San Antonio as part of Depression-era New Deal programs. The card table is set for Dominos. President Johnson's favorite game was 42, and he took every opportunity to play.

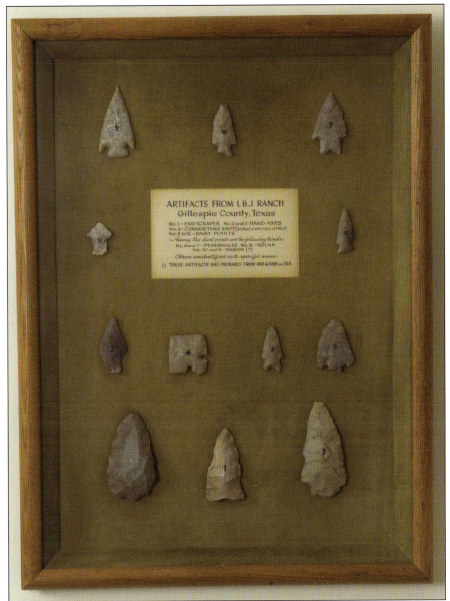 

A favorite story from Lynda is related to the arrowhead collection framed on the wall above the dominos table. Mrs. Johnson had offered one dollar to Lynda and Luci for each arrowhead they found on the ranch. Ever resourceful, Lynda recruited the assistance of local children, who helped her in the quest. As her mama presented a dollar for Lynda's growing contributions to the arrowhead collection, she would share fifty cents with the finder.

DINING ROOM

The first addition to the house included adding eight feet to the dining room, enlarging the kitchen, and adding carport parking in the back. The large picture window provides a view of ranch lands, the Jackson Magnolia (a seedling from the White House tree), and Mrs. Johnson's bird feeders. She delighted in watching grandchildren playing out back.

Countless official and family meals were enjoyed in this room. At times the dining table was expanded and other tables added, allowing for more than twenty to dine. At other times the "breakfast table" positioned under the picture window would suffice. We're not exactly sure when the office chair became a regular fixture, but once Lyndon Johnson realized the extra comfort, an office chair was always there.

Much to Mrs. Johnson's chagrin, a telephone was affixed to one leg of the dining table. His most-used tool, a telephone was never more than a few steps away. With over one hundred phone lines running to the ranch, there were telephones in every room, every building, around the yard, and in his car. Liz Carpenter, Mrs. Johnson's press secretary, once said she thought of LBJ "as a long arm with a telephone at one end of it."

One of my favorite stories was related by an agent of the United States Secret Service. He told me that at the beginning of a meal President Johnson asked his press secretary, Bill Moyers, to return thanks. As Moyers began to pray, President Johnson was recalled to say, "Speak up, Bill, I can't hear you," to which Mr. Moyers replied, "I wasn't speaking to you, Mr. President." The story is a testament to the strong relationship and comradery of the leader and his staff.

Lynda Robb recalled seating arrangements for large groups. "When we had too many to fit at the 'big table,' Luci and I would be seated at the 'children's table'"—the table at the large picture window. "When Chuck [Lynda's husband, Charles Robb] was elected governor of Virginia, I asked if now Chuck got to eat at the big table."

The wallpaper was chosen for its depiction of country scenes. The tall wooden candlesticks were made from banisters from the temporary Texas Capitol and were gifts from Jesse Kellam, the Johnsons' business manager, who operated their Texas Broadcasting Service. Governor and Mrs. John Connally gave the other set. They are copies of Sam Houston's candlesticks. The ornamental soup tureen by Villeroy & Boch (c. 1882–1885) was a gift of close friends.

KITCHEN

This room was restored by the National Park Service to its 1960s appearance. Most features and furnishings in the room are original to the president's time (1963–1973). One of the special things about this house is that through the efforts of the Johnson family, along with wonderful friends of the family and the park, it is presented accurately and authentically.

A pecan pie sits at the stovetop, a reminder of November 23, 1964, when pecan pies were being prepared for a large barbecue in the oak grove to honor President Kennedy. As news of the assassination in Dallas came over the small TV atop the refrigerator; everything stopped, and the transformation began from vice president's home to home of the president of the United States.

DEN

President and Mrs. Johnson's daughters refer to the den as the "crossroads" of the house. This is the room where official guests of the president might join others before a ceremony or press conference being held on the front porch. The place where family members gathered before heading out for a walk or ride. In this room Lyndon and Lady Bird Johnson signed documents gifting the ranch to the National Park Service.

The president liked Fannie Lou Spelce's primitive paintings, and several are displayed in the house. Lynda Robb describes the painting displayed on the den wall as "Mrs. Spelce's imagination of a scene where Daddy is sitting on the front porch of the Birthplace Home. His mother, Rebekah, is in the front yard when his father, Sam E. Johnson Jr., arrives riding a horse."

Audio control boxes sit on tables and are mounted in walls throughout the house. The Johnsons (mostly LBJ) would control music feeds and broadcasts inside and around the yard by choosing a source from the control boxes. Want to listen to their TV or radio stations out of Austin? Just push the button. Want some Muzak? The Johnsons owned the local franchise, and the company made specially selected reel-to-reel tapes to play at the ranch.

THE LARGE WOODEN COFFEE TABLE WAS MADE FROM A 1,400-YEAR-OLD TREE THAT FELL IN SHERWOOD FOREST AND WAS A GIFT OF FRANK STANTON, PRESIDENT OF CBS.

YELLOW SITTING ROOM

This was the eastern-most ground floor room of the ranch house when purchased by the Johnsons in 1951. It served as their bedroom from 1952 to 1967, when it was replaced by the bedroom suites. Due to the size, it's easy to see why Mrs. Johnson wanted Lyndon to have an office.

The Yellow Room today is furnished as it was after the master bedroom additions. It became a room for small meetings and social gatherings. The collection of pencil sketches on the west wall is by Julian Onderdonk, a Texas impressionist painter from San Antonio whose Texas landscapes are highly prized. President George W. Bush displayed three Onderdonk paintings in the Oval Office.

Several head-of-state gifts adorn this room, including the leather hassocks given by the president of Paraguay. Photo albums line bookshelves on one side and contain hundreds of photographs documenting Johnson family history and events from 1934 to 1968.

From these photo albums we were able to learn the meaning of the fifth star on the LBJ Ranch flag. His initials, in cursive as he wrote them, lie on a blue field adorned by five stars. The LBJ stars represent Lyndon Baines Johnson, Lady Bird Johnson, Lynda Bird Johnson, and Luci Baines Johnson, with the fifth for Little Beagle Johnson.

The Porfirio Salinas painting was a Christmas gift to Senator Lyndon Johnson from his staff. Salinas was another of the Johnsons' favorite Texas artists.

Julian Onderdonk sketch

PRESIDENT'S BATHROOM

THE PRESIDENT'S COLOGNES AND TOILETRY ITEMS REMAIN ON THE SHELVES MUCH AS HE LEFT THEM.

PRESIDENT'S BEDROOM

According to Luci and Lynda, "Mama and Daddy shared a bedroom throughout Daddy's life." What Mrs. Johnson had learned of her work-driven husband was that it would be important to have a place to escape when the phone calls and meetings were occurring well beyond midnight or long before dawn.

President Johnson loved the Pedernales River, a place that provided fond memories since his youth. When the curtains were back, he had an inspiring view of the river. These scenes would be the last he would know, as he passed away in the room on January 22, 1973. In his last month, the family, his doctors, and friends had grown increasingly concerned. LBJ had often referred to the mortality of the "Johnson men," recalling that his father had died at sixty. LBJ had nearly died of a massive heart attack before his forty-seventh birthday. At sixty-four years of age, he had outlived his father, but the stresses of his political life, bad eating habits, years of smoking, and repeated twelve-plus-hour workdays had taken their toll on his body.

He knew four grandchildren. Madam Shoumatoff, who painted the official White House portraits of LBJ and Lady Bird, was commissioned to paint three of them. Next to the bed is Nicole Nugent, Luci's second born. On the east wall are paintings of Lyndon Nugent, Luci's first child and an ever-present figure in photos with his grandfather. Next to Lyndon is Lucinda Robb, Lynda's first child. Catherine Robb, Lynda's second daughter, was the youngest (at time of the president's death) and sadly did not have her portrait painted.

Left to right: Nicole, Lyndon, Lucinda

A telephone with intercom is attached to the bedside table. Retired United States Secret Service agent Mike Howard recalls that LBJ, always connected, uttered his last words, "Get me Mike, get me Mike!" on this phone. Unfortunately, the efforts of many on that fateful day could not save the president's life from a massive heart attack.

Like most proud grandparents, Lyndon B. Johnson displayed artwork from his granddaughter, Lynda's daughter, Lucinda Robb (Cindy) and grandson, Luci's son Lyndon. Both drawings continue to hang in the bedroom, taped to the wall.

The large paintings on walls closest to the bed depict scenes beloved by Lyndon Johnson. One shows the home and cattle operation of his grandfather, Sam E. Johnson Sr., in Johnson City; the other is of the Sauer-Beckman Farm across the river in the LBJ State Park and Historic Site. Grandson Lyndon Nugent's drawing of an airplane. Lyndon served as a pilot in the U.S. Army and has enjoying a lifetime of flying helicopters and airplanes occasionally flying to and from the LBJ Ranch airstrip.

The three TVs, a feature of the Texas White House and the White House, allowed LBJ to watch all three networks at the same time. If you visit Elvis's Graceland home in Memphis, you'll see the same setup in his media room. The Graceland guide told me Elvis was inspired by LBJ.

The massage table, a regular feature in the room when the president was in residence, dominates one side of the room. He often had a massage and short nap in the afternoon before continuing with the workday, which typically went well into the night.

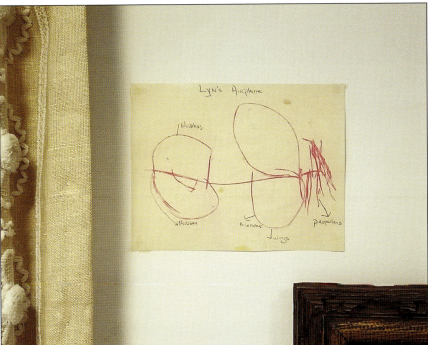

Leaving the president's bedroom, you get a second view of the hallway. This view looks back to the den. The photographs on the walls depict moments and important people who figured prominently in the very public lives of the Johnsons. Dozens of influential political and industrial leaders' images hang beside christening photos of grandchildren.

Mrs. Johnson's 2004 Christmas card shows eight of her great-grandchildren. As with Luci and Lynda, the grandchildren and great-grandchildren enjoyed countless visits and memories at the LBJ Ranch with their Nini. Mrs. Johnson outlived her husband by thirty-four years and found delight in seven grandchildren and ten great grandchildren. The ranch and their Nini figured prominently in their lives until her death in 2007. At the time of this publication, four additional great-grandchildren have blessed the Johnson family.

MRS. JOHNSON'S BEDROOM SUITE

Lady Bird's bedroom appears as she left it in July 2007. Used for study, reflection, conversation, reading, and rest, this room was her place to escape from the daily pressures that came with being a First Lady, businesswoman, mother, and grandmother.

The president wanted a view of the river, and Mrs. Johnson wanted to look upon her gardens. You won't see the display of flowers today, as there are no twenty-four-hour guards to keep away hungry deer, but the east door allowed her to quickly access her flower beds, the 1955 outdoor pool, and the indoor pool she had built in 1989. A girl from east Texas, she grew up around rivers and lakes. She loved the water and swam nearly every day.

Mrs. Johnson's bathroom.

Some of the ranch house furnishings were purchased for the Elms, the Johnsons' home while LBJ served as vice president (there was no official residence at that time). Personal furnishings were moved to the family residence at the White House and again to the Texas White House in 1969.

Shelves filled with books throughout the house reflect Mrs. Johnson's love of reading. President Johnson spent his life reading government reports and memos while Lady Bird lost herself in a wide variety of books. A University of Texas graduate with two degrees, her love of journalism reflected a desire to learn and explore and led to hundreds of photographs and home movies. Her degree in history inspired a passion for America's natural and cultural past and a devotion to conserving and saving public places for future generations.

Along with books are prints, paintings, and figurines of birds. I had to laugh when Lynda exclaimed, "Oh, poor Mama, with a name like Lady Bird everyone felt they needed to give her something with a bird on it." On the lower shelves are two important items: a Browning camera, a gift from LBJ, and a tape recorder used by Mrs. Johnson when she was recording thoughts at the ranch. Recorded memories, impressions, and events of the presidential years would become her book, A White House Diary, which she began on November 22, 1963.

There are many embroidered pillows throughout the house. These decorative pillows on her bed beautifully describe our beloved Lady Bird Johnson.

Mrs. Johnson's desk was used at their home in Washington, D.C. and in the White House before its placement in her bedroom. All her work spaces included pictures of family and close friends. Often papers and correspondence overflowed onto the floor where they could be processed and handled by assistants.

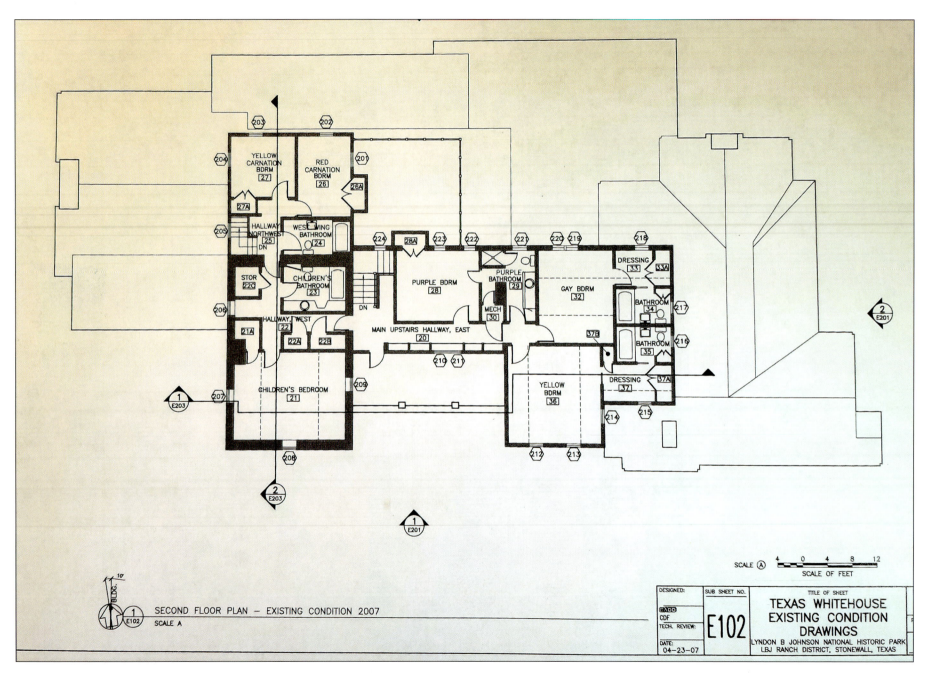

THE SECOND FLOOR (Stairs leading upstairs from the den.)

63

CHILDREN'S BEDROOM

Above the living room, part of the original 1894 stone house, is the children's bedroom. Friends of Luci and Lynda occasionally overnighted in this room, as did guests of the family such as Laurance and Mary Rockefeller. The grandchildren have fond memories of evenings spent in this room playing, visiting with friends and cousins, dressing, and sleeping. Lynda and daughter Lucinda spent time in this room while her husband, Charles Robb, was serving in Vietnam.

WEST HALLWAY BATHROOMS

Over the dining room and living room are two full bathrooms. The green and pink bathroom was one of the first with running water in Gillespie County. When Judge Clarence and wife Frank Martin first installed the bathroom, it is said that they opened the house on Sunday afternoons so local folks could see this marvel of modern convenience.

The second bathroom tub overflowed (a result of grandchildren?), and water ran down the south wall of the dining room, permanently staining the wallpaper. Mrs. Johnson's solution was to have an art student paint more clouds.

CARNATION BEDROOMS

The two small Carnation Bedrooms started as one large master bedroom for LBJ's aunt and uncle Martin. These bedrooms were intended for house staff, but they were often reassigned to meet an increasing need to accommodate guests.

Some real creativity went into making closet space in these rooms by removing windows and building boxes extending out from the exterior wall.

PURPLE BEDROOM & BATH

Moving down the hallway to the east is the Purple Bedroom. Adorned in flowered paper on the walls and ceiling, it was a popular bedroom with its own bathroom adjoining. The bedroom usually accommodated whoever was serving as President Johnson's secretary.

YOUNG CLAUDIA ALTA TAYLOR (LADY BIRD).

PURPLE BEDROOM'S ADJOINING BATHROOM.

MASTER GUEST BEDROOM & BATH

My favorite upstairs bedroom was known by me as the Kennedy Bedroom. Also known as the Yellow Poppy Bedroom, it was enjoyed by many notable guests such as President-Elect John F. Kennedy, Speaker of the House Sam Rayburn, and two West German chancellors. In the 1960s the room was known as the Green Room. Obviously Mrs. Johnson had it redecorated later.

GAY FLOWER BEDROOM & BATH

The Gay Flower Bedroom has the most memorable wallpaper. Mrs. Johnson called it gay because entering brought a smile to the guest's face.

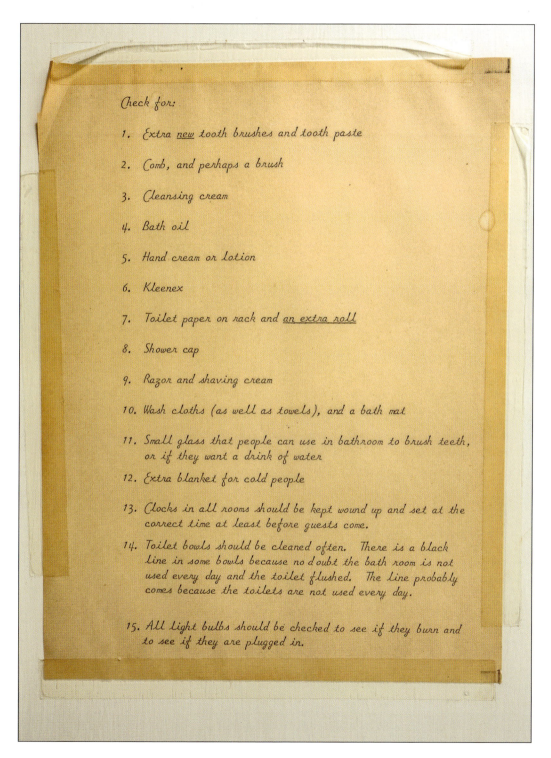

The bedrooms and baths on the second floor still seem to echo with laughter and conversation of family and guests from that time. The rooms are still furnished with original pieces and hold many fond memories for family and friends. Grandchildren wandered these halls and played in rooms where world leaders had visited. The Texas White House was very much both official residence and family home.

Luci Johnson summed it up for me during a tour for friends. As she stepped over the ropes and picked up an embroidered pillow, she looked at me, grinned, and told the group that the National Park Service now treats the house like a museum, but to the Johnsons it was the playground for children and a wonderful place for family to gather.

There remains on an upstairs wall Mrs. Johnson's checklist reminding her staff of supplies and actions to be taken in preparation for guests.

Mrs. Johnson was known for her graciousness and caring. Her executive assistant, Shirley James, told me that Mrs. Johnson "put great store" in being a good hostess and periodically spent the night in each of the "company" bedrooms to ensure her guests would be comfortable and have everything needed for an enjoyable stay in the ranch house.

VIEW FROM UPSTAIRS FRONT PORCH

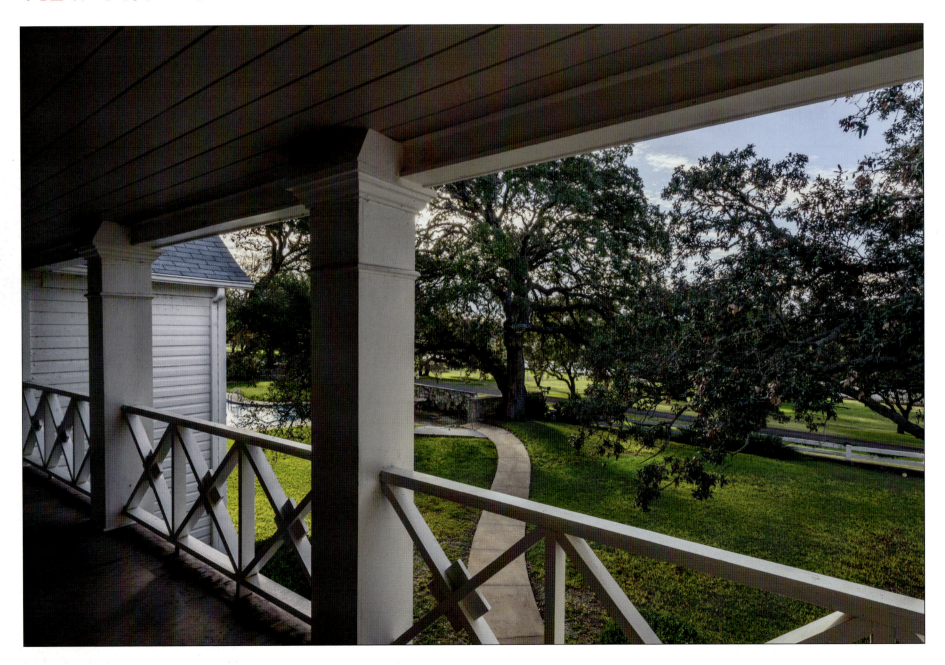

A ramshackle house and overgrown pastures transformed and grew as Senate majority leader became vice president and then president. As Lyndon Johnson's political power and influence grew, the Johnsons recognized an ongoing need to improve facilities, houses, infrastructure, roadways, and staffing on the LBJ Ranch. The improvements served President Johnson and his First Lady well. The ranch increasingly became a regular site on national news and elevated the Texas Hill Country to a familiar region for many Americans.

A line of red granite tombstones marks the final resting place of Lyndon B. Johnson and his grandparents, parents, siblings, and wife. The fame has passed: aircraft no longer circle waiting to land; notable individuals and world leaders are not a regular occurrence. What does remain are the ranch lands, clean air, and flowing waters of the Pedernales, and places that brought a president strength, inspiration, and pride.

"NO ONE COULD EVER UNDERSTAND LYNDON JOHNSON UNLESS THEY UNDERSTOOD THE LAND AND THE PEOPLE FROM WHICH HE CAME. THE LAND IS HERE, THE PEOPLE ARE HERE. HIS ROOTS WERE DEEP RIGHT HERE ON THIS SPOT IN THE HILL COUNTRY."
—REV. BILLY GRAHAM

August 27, 1990. Mrs. Johnson with Luci Baines Johnson and husband Ian Turpin accompanied by some of their children and a military representative.

Each year the National Park Service and United States military representatives hold a wreath-laying ceremony on the president's birthday, August 27. Mrs. Johnson began the tradition of a short ceremony in 1973 after the president's death that January. President Johnson issued orders to have military representatives begin placing a wreath at the grave of former presidents on their birthday.

THE PILLOW WAS A GIFT OF NITA LOUISE MAYO, THE DAUGHTER OF JESSIE KELLAM, LONG-TIME MANAGER OF THE JOHNSONS' BROADCASTING INTERESTS AND CLOSE PERSONAL FAMILY FRIEND.

March 2018: Charles Spenser Robb, son of Jennifer Robb and Josh Glazer, great-grandson of Lyndon B. Johnson and Claudia Taylor Johnson, is ready for his first ride in the LBJ 100 Bicycle Tour. Charles's participation in the ride demonstrates that, as Aunt Luci says, "generations of Johnsons" continue to support the national historical park that manages some of the family's most precious gifts.

IMAGE CREDITS

Front Cover, 11, 15, 16, 19, 22, 23, 24, 26, 27, 30, 34, 37, 38, 44, 45-Onderdonk, 46, 47, 49, 50, 52, 54, 56, 61, 64, 65, 67, 68, 69, 70, 71, 73, 74, 75, 76, 77, 78, 80, 82, 85 © Scot Miller/ScotMiller.com

20-21, 25, 29, 35, 36, 40, 41, 42, 45, 51, 53-TV's, 58, 59, 60, 63. David Valdez, by Lyndon B. Johnson National Historical Park and Friends of LBJ National Historical Park

18, 62. National Park Service, Historic Structure Report, Texas White House

iv-v, 2, 3, 39-controller, back cover Russ Whitlock

4, 10. Courtesy Shelton Coleman from personal collection of Melvin and Anita Winters

5, 6, 7, 8, 9, 12, 13, 14, 28, 32, 43, 55, 79, 81, 85-LBJ in pool. LBJ Presidential Library

17, 31-arrowheads, 39-Spelce, 43-flag, 48, 53, 57-drawing, 66, 72. Lyndon B. Johnson National Historical Park

1, 27-Luci & Ian, 83 Courtesy of Johnson family. Permission for photographs of personal belongings and paintings included in this book is granted by Luci Baines Johnson and Lynda Johnson Robb

The Lyndon B. Johnson National Historical Park of Johnson City and Stonewall is a perfect complement to the LBJ Presidential Library and Lady Bird Johnson Wildflower Center in Austin, the LBJ State Park and Historic Site in Stonewall, and the LBJ Museum San Marcos. Each tells important stories of their life and legacy. But nowhere can you more intimately know the Johnsons than walking through their home. Mrs. Johnson's desire was that "the house look like we've just gone out for a drive around the ranch." Lynda Johnson Robb and Luci Baines Johnson, daughters of the president and Mrs. Johnson, along with several grandchildren, have ensured the house is originally furnished and representative of the president's time.

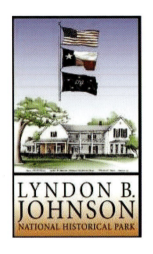

The 1955 swimming pool addition became a favorite spot for official and family gatherings. Mrs. Johnson had the pool constructed after LBJ's near fatal heart attack to encourage exercise.

President Johnson reading a memo while holding Yuki as grandson Lyndon Nugent looks on.

This photo, taken by Ian Turpin in October 2006, with Mrs. Johnson, Libby and Barney Hulett, and Luci Johnson, began my "adoption" into the Johnson family. Through ten years of service as park superintendent, I became increasingly thirsty for information and details about the thirty-sixth president and his incredible First Lady. I'm thrilled to share photos and stories of the Texas White House and the family that called it home for fifty-six years. Members of the Johnson family continue to inspire many by doing good for the benefit of others.

My heartfelt thanks to Luci Johnson and Lynda Robb, Shirley James, Shelton Coleman, Matt Wigglesworth, Scot Miller, and my NPS friends for their assistance in making this book the best it could be.